# From The Rhyming Realm of Gandolin

## Volume One:

## Ghosts In Jars

D. B. Feister

:THE MINES OF GLORFINDORIUM:
"THE CAPPS"
ICE WORLD CITY
GHOST TOWN
THE WESTLANDS
HARBORTOWNE
"SERPENTS FANG ISLE"
THE MILL
STED
"THE TOWN BY THE RIVER"
TOWERTOWN
FLOODPLAIN BAY
OWNLEE GATE
N
NW
NE
W
E
G

# CONTENTS

Part 1: Ghosts In Jars      Page 1

Part 2: Birth of the Hunt   Page 20

Part 3: Debt Sentence      Page 77

# GHOSTS IN JARS

A cloak with a hood

Gold cross and a jar,

This night is as black

As freshly mixed tar.

The wind's bite is crisp

Trees whispering words

But speak with a lisp

Unlike eloquent birds.

Leaves, which are dead

Crunch under the feet

Of a thundering horse

A magnificent steed.

The task, it is drawn

The job, it is clear

Tonight, it's a man

That the spirits will fear.

With old, withered hands

Gripped tight on the reins

He flies down the road

Like he's going insane…


Who knew that ghosts,

Could be sold for a buck?

Well they can, and it's said

That a specter brings luck.

So hunters set out

From near, and from far

To hunt down some haunters

And trap them in jars.

Bring them to markets

And place them on shelves

With stickers that read:

IMPORTED FROM HELL.

Tho first, he'll need cargo

Master Garbool has run out

So assigned he has been

To take part in these bouts…

An aged, empty manor

Alone on a hill

Housed uneasy souls

Of the men who were killed.

Twas a terrible feud

Between father and son

One nabbed a knife

While one grabbed a gun.

A bullet met muscle

As "blast!" filled the air,

with father soon dead

Fore the fight was not fair.

Fair?

Very few duels are fair,

It's tough to match up an identical pair.

So, as one sided battles

Turned bloody affair

A man filled his wallet

Snaring souls from the air.

Though, tonight I'm afraid

A man's met his match

Oh the gheists in this place

Were a mean, vengeful batch.

Before door he enters

Lips whispered a prayer

A plea for safeguard

From unholy despair…

The weathered, wood gate

Creaked as it whined

As a threshold was crossed

Then a door slammed behind.

Now, this veteran hunter

Would never admit

Nervousness felt

Stomach forming a pit.

Sweat dropped from his face

As breaths became short

Cuz solo he'd gone

To this spiritual fort…

Outta nowhere, a screech

Sent waves through the black

Then poltergeist showed

As a shadow stepped back.

With courage, it yelled

A shout from its mouth

"JAR, TRAP THIS FIEND

AND DON'T LET IT OUT!"

Then like a magnet

Joins two different ores

The ghost filled the glass,

A spiritual score.

One phantom fenced,

Tho plenty to go

Invisible now

But soon, they would show…

The man looked at his catch

Frozen trapped in a bottle

If seal and soul broke

His neck would be throttled.

The cork to the jar

was tied down with rope

he had purchased from nuns

who said, "Blessed by the Pope."

"True? …who knows?

He thought as he smirked

All he'd known of the twine

Was well, that fine stuff worked.

A timber wolf's howl

Sent chills down his spine

As trees shook outside

The elms, oaks, and pines…


Lightning shot down

For all it was worth

Winds became Gaels

Ripping roots from the earth.

Yet, all seemed at peace

In the creepy, white mansion

While storm outside swelled

With explosive expansion…

His keen eye caught sight

Of a strange, floating light

That shined, dipped, and darted

As it danced in the night.

It hovered above

His head, did the ghost

Tho our seeker stood still

Never leaving his post.

Then just as before

The shouting, again

And just as before

The specter was penned.

"These first two, too easy"

He thought to himself

Then imagined the profits

Full jars packing his shelves.

Holding tight to those prizes

He should have been done

If reverse time he could

He would go back, and run...

Fore a monster dwelled here

And was near to appear

That could anytime fill

Any soul up with fear.

Twas the ghost of the father

Who was killed by the gun

That was fired in feud

By his only born son.

This made his spirit

Angry and sad

Still clutching the blade

Still armored and clad.

Our hunter, aware

This old hand wasn't dumb

Yes, the cursed ghostly jackpot

Was the reason he'd come.

This now wraith, once warlord

Was known all around

For taking out hunters

Who trespassed his grounds.

Most, wouldn't dare

Stuck to much weaker ghosts

Sure their coffers weren't crammed

But they weren't to be toast…

Numerical bounties

Were placed very high

For the ghastliest boss

Of that castles inside.

Now that is just why

It's our charge's desire

If one scores and survives

Then that man could retire.

With mountains of coin

Made of gold jagaroons

He could claim an estate

Hell, and twelve flocks of loons!

So greed brought him forth

On a crisp, autumn night

About to be served

Eight hot plates of fight.

The weather, now raging

Did sonic winds fly

Thunderbolts flashed, cracked

And blew up the sky.

Then all of the might

Seemed to gather as one

Formed an energy beam

Twice as bright as the sun..

The light dropped from the heavens

And down through the clouds

Then vanished from sight

As it shot in the house.

Then, that napping abode woke

Fore its master was here

To quell an intruder

Whose heart knew few fears.

Our hunter looked on

Wide eyed at that scene

Which destroyed his demeanor

Wiping confidence clean.

For a very long while

Twas the first time he'd felt

Terror take his mind

And it squeezed like a belt.

The beat of his soul

Got faster and grew

Till his motor's loud pumps

Could be heard through the room...

In this hall, every object

Now shimmered with light

A pulsing green vibe

that hindered his sight.

A flash, and a blast

Sent light through the room

Filling eyes and ears

With a very bright, "BOOM!"

He lay on the ground

Now blind as a bat

Couldn't even detect

Where his ghost bottles sat.

Fear, oh wonderful fear

Makes neck hair stand tall

And fills eyes with tears

Tho, no need for a mirror

For his vision was perfectly clear…

Though optics now donned a disguise

A solid, black mask

Now covered his eyes

He'd rather have died.

As he scrambled he learned

It was just as he feared

Not only his eyes

But also his ears.

Silent, salty drops

Dripped down on the boots

Of the doomed in the dark

In a world that was mute…

The ghost had done nothing

But had easily won

With the fight being done

Fore he'd had any fun.

So it drifted away

As the hunter just crawled

Lost in a maze

With invisible walls.

Starvation took hold

And soon he did pass

Trapped, was his soul

In the house he would last.

Someday, new blood

This way would pass

Maybe catching his ghost

In a bottle of glass.

Then, sold as a charm

For a very good price

The cycle keeps on

Each day and each night.

Hunters go out

From near, and from far

Who, if are not careful

Might end up in a jar...

# GHOSTS IN JARS II:
# BIRTH OF THE HUNT

A mariner's bell

Rang loud and rang clear

As boat after ship

Came to dock at the pier.

Captains made their return

From faraway lands

With great foreign goods

Matching spender's demands.

Thousands of crates

Would arrive every day

Unloaded at port

To be sold in this way.

All this land's items

Were to meet in one space

Harbortowne's world famous

Street marketplace.

For one young urchin

Today was the day

Twas the time he would learn

His good father's way.

How to bargain and haggle

To wheel and to deal

Get so much for so little

He'd effectively steal…

The boy and his father

Entered the gate

And at once, joined the mob

Who awaited the freight.

They could hear music,

Loud and alive

And smell every restaurant

The spots, and the dives.

The people were endless

Many voices, one chant

The wave's moves, robotic

Like an army of ants...

Harbortowne... heart of this world

And in that, with but one lake

Cities like these

Weren't meant to be plural.

The soul of the planet

The tunes, games, and food

Kept all of the ants

In a very fine mood.

Tho, back to the kid

And his businessman dad

whom stuck in his mind

one item it had.

A brand new sensation

Had swept all around

Stores simply claimed,

"we're all fresh out!" …

There were none to be found.

After hours spent searching

The son finally asked

Just why they had come

To these shops in these shacks…

The father said nothing

Eyes peering a sign

That caught his attention

Tugged his mind on a line.

Then the two entered

This back alley shop

For this, their last hope

Was one's most, likely stop.

A clueless boy followed

Step by step in the shack

As flimsy doors flapped

And snapped at his back…

Scores of odd objects

He'd never imagined

Now filled his vision

Some were sure to be magic.

He looked to the corner

And spied a huge cage

Which contained a large bird

That shrieked, full of rage.

Its eyes looked like rubies

Red as fresh blood

And its feathers were brown

As if coated in mud.

Though the raptor was strange

There were much weirder things

From ogre face masks

To dragon bone rings.

From a "witch's hair" toothbrush

To bleached goblin skulls

This shop was the best

This shop had it all…

As his eyes looked around

His ears heard a noise

That crackled and gasped,

Twas an ancient man's voice.

26

The child wheeled 'round

And saw the old geezer

More wrinkles than teeth

An old, weasly weezer.

His lungs, it did seem

Were coated in dust

Because in between breaths

In his hacks, you could trust.

His fingers resembled

Aged, withered twigs

His beady eyes, hungry

Like two cunning pigs.


This was Garbool

The shop keeping king

His financial goal?

To get every coin that you'd bring.

Clever persuasion

Mixed with years on the job

Let him outwit them all

Leaving most to be robbed…

But the father, no fool

Had known of Garbool

How he ripped off the best

How he took most to school.

The best course of action

Take coin pouch, and lock it

Attempt to steer clear

From the mental pick-pocket.

The father, leaned forward

While son stood behind

Then asked old Garbool

If a ghost, they could find…

First, only silence

Then a smile was cracked

A gnarled, nasty grin

Baring rotten teeth black.

"Ghosts?" he replied

In his elderly hiss

"Bottled like wine,

From the vines of abyss?"

The father just nodded

Was this one of his games?

If not careful this creton

Would make fool of his brain.

"Ya know, it seems"

He spat as he coughed

"My spiritual shipments

Have really dropped off."

"I haven't a ghost

On not one of my shelves"

Garbool was sincere

And the father could tell.

But the crafty, old coot

Wasn't through with his tricks

His mind's gears were grinding

Forming schemes as they clicked…

"This man and his boy"

He thought in his head

"Might have what it takes,

To capture the dead…

Yes, send them away

With all they will need

Two hunters for hire

Fetching spirits for me…"

As early as recent

His last decent guy tried

Tho he picked the wrong fight

Got his butt kicked, and died.

Now of course, they'd be paid

Yes, he still had a heart

But his piece of the pie

Would be most of the tart.

The keeper and his kept

Were poor to be sure

Neither had jobs,

Yet their spirits were pure.

This made them perfect,

Real regular Joes

If they failed and were slayed

Well, no skin off his nose…

Handshakes were shook

And papers were signed

Then father and son

Left the strange shop behind.

Lightly equipped

With supplies and a map

They traveled due south

To a town by "The Caps".

These hills formed a range

Of mountains so high

That the snow on their peaks

Seemed to whiten the sky…

During their trip

They checked out their gear

All the gadgets and tools

That would aid them out here.

There were ten glass jars

All perfect in shape

And two savage blades

That could cut down an ape.

Inside of the bag

Lay some rope, thin as floss

And just for good measure

They were given a cross.

Other than food

And the clothes on their backs

This was all that they carried

And all that they had…

They were told, "ghosts are simple"

Even, "easy for fools"

Just fill up ten jars

And return to Garbool.

A rusty, red sign

Squeaked and swayed in the wind

That read in bold print,

"WELCOME ALL, WHO HAVE

SINNED."

This grim, mining town

Now mostly abandoned

Was once quite the buzz

Filled with people and wagons.

Tho these days twas barren

Fore the villagers chose

To exit this place

After most the mines closed.

So our two virgin hunters

Came to desolate streets

Searching and hoping

For ghosts they would meet…

But a problem they had

With no answer to match

How would a soul

These jars manage to catch?

So they dumped out the contents

Of their pack on the ground

As the knives, rope, and bottles

Fell and scattered around.

Then as if out of nowhere

There floated a shred

Of parchment with stamps,

And writing that said…

*"Hello fools!*

*It is I, Garbool*

*Here to explain*

*These magical tools.*

*We'll start with those jars*

*They never will crack*

*Fore them are designed*

*To stop ghosts in their tracks.*

*Just open the seal*

*When a spirit is near*

*Point bottle at beast*

*And don't show no fear.*

*But in order to score*

*You must shout from your mouth,*

*"JAR TRAP THIS FIEND*

*AND DON'T LET IT OUT!"*

*Those nine words are special*

*A mystical spell*

*Designed to Imprison*

*Illusions from hell.*

*Next, comes the rope*

*Which you surely should use*

*Fore when jar seal meets twine*

*They will magically fuse.*

*That line will ensure*

*The safest of bets*

*A real safety net*

*That will bring you success.*

*And lastly, those knives*

*Cuz well, don't be scared*

*But the place you are now*

*Is infested with bears...*

*I hope what I've wrote*

*Will shed light on your quest*

*Now, go catch some ghosts*

*And give it your best!"*

As the last word was read

It was oh so cliché

When a mighty wind blew

And the note flew away.

So, they picked out a house

At the end of the road

That was likely abandoned

By flesh, blood, and bone.

A door was kicked in

Then silence was heard

But due swiftly shattered

By shrieks, like a bird.

The two looked and saw

Near an old, wooden post

Afloat in the air

Was a small, shiny ghost.

Neither father nor son

Had seen what they saw

Neck hairs now stood

And their courage was gone.

The young boy stood back

With a frozen, still heart

But watched as his dad

Pulled the jar seal apart…

Then, he aimed right his bottle

And screamed from his mouth,

"Jar, trap this fiend

And don't let it out!"

A flash, and a gasp

Was swept through the room

Winds lifted and smacked

The kid's head with a broom.

But the father now smiled

Yes, held in his grasp

An angry, caged ghost

Tied down with rope clasped.

Our two rookie hunters

Now, way past belief

Just nervously grinned

And sighed in relief.

Their first unit made

Sure, that was fine

But more work was in need

Add their one catch, plus nine.

They proceeded to search

Till the whole house was clear

Then left, and went out

To induce some more fear…

Tho, the more ghosts they saw

The better they fared

Till it got to the point

That of ghosts they weren't scared.

They scowered the mill

And stalked every alley

Till nine was the number

Of souls in their tally.

Nine, only nine…

They must get one more

Ten bottles of phantom

Was what they'd come for.

However, an issue

They had searched the whole town

And it seemed they had caught

Every ghost to be found…

Night was approaching

With its blanketing blight

As the duo spied light

That laid far off in sight.

After drawn to the flame

With instinctive desire,

They found them a cabin

With a hot, roaring fire…

Through the windows they glared

And saw with their stares

A wrinkly, old woman

Just rocking her chair.

She, the first human

They'd seen in a week

Was this gentle, old crone

So calm and so meek.

"knock-knock" went a fist

Upon the oak door

"Please, let us in!

We are hungry, and sore!"

But the withered, hag sat

Not a muscle she moved

As the sway from her throne

Never strayed from its groove.

Then strangely, the latch

Where most times a key

You'd need to unlock

Clicked by itself… "What trick could this be?"

That was the thought

Of a truly shocked man

But bitter, cold winds

Made for quick choice of plan.

As he reached for the knob

It turned on its own

With a slow, creaking slide

The home's insides were shown.

Marvelous woodwork

Every cabinet? Top shelf

To a gigantic mirror

Hung to gaze at one's self.

Pictures of graves

Were well, "creepy" you'd call

Scattered in random

Nailed spots on the wall.

Still, all the while

Like a statue she sat,

But heard, were the purrs

From her lap resting cat.

I believe, "perplexed"

Twas the most proper word

One could use to describe

Two whose voice was now slurred.

"Uhmm… Hello.." said the boy

"Can I… uh… sit in your chair?"

Tho the dame didn't budge

She just kept up her stare…

Icy, blue eyes

Looked ahead, oh so cold

A tale soaked in grief

Was the story they told.

"Excuse me, ma'am

But while we are here
Could you spare any rations,
And maybe… a beer?"
As the father's mouth stopped
Cuz he'd finished his talking
His ears caught "pit-pat"
Four-pawed, feline stalking.
Yes, walking right up
Was the jet black, fur coated
Formerly napping cat
Who then quoted…

"I'm sorry, old chaps
But my lady is gone
Yes, the body remains
Tho her soul has been pawned."

Awe coursed throughout

The veins of our two,

A speaking house-mouser?

Had their sanities flew?

It was true, cuz in fact

Before their own eyes

A whiskered one

Shook its head, and then sighed…

"I knew you'd be shocked…

Now pick up your jaws!

I too was once human…"

As he licked near his claws.

"Two years and three months

To the day, in a week

Ago, we did own

This house by that creek.

However, a demon

From pentagram came

Then left the whole town

Mixed, twisted, and lame.

Most folk were killed

Or their spirits done stoled

Or switched up with beasts

As from posted hosts pulled.

Men who were struck

Swapped souls with the swine

Ran mad, to the wild

Squealing in time.

Dead-of-night black

Clouds swirled to our home

Straight towards the door

That dark creature roamed.

With a whisper of words

And two magical zaps

My wife's soul he stole

And I woke as this cat…

Yes, when I came to

Fur covered my face

While the life from my wife

Was then gone with no trace.

So now I reside

With breath, fresh of mice

Haven't ate me no beef

Haven't tasted one spice.

A chef, I once was

And I know this sounds dumb

But you can't grill a steak

When you don't have no thumbs…

In fact, you're the first

Folk I've seen since that day

When every last piece

Of my world went away…"

Silence then echoed

All through the house

But quickly was broke

By the scurries of mouse.

"Ahh, forget it" he purred

"By the way, call me Jack"

As our two rookie hunters

Sat, stunned at these facts.

"Can we sleep here?"

The father then spoke

"Yes you may" replied Jack

"On the rung, hang your cloaks."

That night was the most

Strange time of their lives

Seemed both had been stabbed

By two mystical knives.

Just one more fenced phantom

Was needed to meet

Their quota for pay

Then Garbool they would greet.

With morning, came calls

From the earliest birds

As a cold, northern winds

Brisk whistles were heard…

After some breakfast

Was scraped from the larder

Our slightly less green

Ghost hunters departed.

"So long" said old Jack

"But please, hear my plea

If encounter that beast

Just promise you'll flee."

By beast, he meant demon

And that demon was "Boke"

Fore it could endanger

The baddest of bloke…

So they wandered due west

At the sight of a chapel

That oversaw shacks

And black hills full of gravel.

Their logic, of course

What better a church?

The gateway to heaven

Must be, where ghouls lurk…

A giant, old bell

Atop of the steeple

Rang loud… even though

No managing people.

Step after step

Was scaled till the top

When peak was then reached

They looked back, and stopped.

"Listen, my son"

The grizzled man spoke

"This ghostly black market

Is far from a joke."

The boy, only nodded

Understanding, yet scared

So far, they'd done well

Yes, till now, greatly fared.

But something felt off

At this threshold of faith

Which stank strong of specter

And reeked ripe of wraith.

Once deep inside

There was no turning back

As two shadows crept

Down the tiles so cracked.

Ducking through aisles

A torch lit the way

Showing dust covered pews

That had seen better days...

Pillars of marble

Holding temple upright

They shined, once splashed

With that fiery light.

Haunting, no doubt

But where was the prize?

Had their gut led them wrong?

Sold their minds a fat lie?

Further was wandered

Yonder toward golden alter

As creaking sounds drowned

Their prayers for no falter...

One foot on that perch

Seemed to switch up the vibe

As windows and doors

Closed or opened up wide.

A ghastly green mist

It fizzled and hissed

Fogging out tables and chairs,

This "sure-to-fright" sight

Made shivering right

Yeah, quivering scared were the pair.

Then, two feeble stares

Got forced to wood seats

Invisibly pushed by the air,

With back-to-bench bend

And courage done spent

The only thing standing was hair.

Suddenly, shapes

Appeared near and far

See through transparent

Yet shined like the stars.

Eye sockets, empty

With bearded face molds

Chanting and ranting

With frigid souls, cold…

A couple of on looking

Choms peed their pants

With each passing tick

Their fear was enhanced.

A duo of emerald figures

Marched, ever more near

Strolling the aisles with a

Stalking style silent as deer.

The tenth, only vacant

Bottle sat tight

As its holder forgot

Its existence that night.

Dropping temps chilled

Killed the warmth of the room

As the poltergeists gathered

Near a plaque that read, "tomb".

A golden slab door

Blocked a tunnel away

Where it led, only dead

Knew how mountain paths stray…

All at once, the ground shook

As the slab rolled aside

While the ghosts of the church

Moved within with a glide.

Soon after, the grasp

That squeezed hunters in bite

Let our rookies go free

Without slightest of fights.

They stood up and ran

But the door wouldn't budge

Madness coursed through

Messing minds to a sludge.

Helplessly heaving

Till panting were lungs

They'd entered a hive

D.B. Feister

And were sure to be stung…

Trapped… like rats in a cage

Or bats in a cave,

Who seem to have lost

Ec-ho-Lo-Cating waves.

For the very first time

In his decade of years

The boy watched his father

Drip salty drop tears.

Optical rain

With a taste like the sea

Formed puddles quite quick

As they fell, weep by weep…

"We're not gonna make it…"

A child's ear snatched

"Soon, they'll return…"

As squeals peeled from a latch.

Over their shoulders

Nearly next to the tomb

A wooden trap door

Opened widely its womb.

Fearing to wait

as bait for the ghosts

This new, hopeful choice

Forced the two to make most.

To be toast, was to stay

So again, the torch blazed

Fire, their guide

Lit their road to escape.

They ducked in the hole

Tumbling down in fall,

When on ground they looked 'round

Spying trio of under earth halls.

One slightly angled

Toward hell it declined

The others went left

What a strangely clutch find!

The choice of which route

They would take was made clear

By a breeze blowing soft

From the path to their rear…

"Surely this wind

Will guide us to haven!"

The dad said as torch

Pierced the dark, black as ravens.

Pace started slow

Though fear brought the haste

Till worries made hurried

Scurries to run from that place.

After some while

The gusts rose again

As did low, chanting drums

Humming beats in the den.

Suddenly, light

Pierced its way to their eyes

Then relief briefly flowed

In two long, drawn out sighs.

But out of the woods

They clearly were not

When vibrant green ghosts

Lit up where they had got.

"How could this be!?!"

Dad wondered aloud

"We walked five miles

At least, underground!"

High up on cliffhanger

Overlooking the chamber

That room, which away

They had ran.

Now down just below

A spiritual show…

At least front row views

Are quite grand…

A dozen monk-shaped

Green figures faced north

Grunting guttural groans

Evil echoes of sort.

A five pointed star

Appeared in the air

Golden in hue

As our two only stared.

Like a Kodiak bear

Snarls at one's face

Their haunting hymn hums

Held a bitter, clawed taste…

Then black mist seeped forth

And the wind howled with might

Now, an event

Yes, a most frightful sight.

When skin turns dead white

It just isn't right

On this night, like a kite's

Snapping string while in flight.

Oh, a fight

That just might

End with a friend

And a foe's dusty bite…

Then twelves monks turned vapor

Ghastly fumes in the room

As a giant black shadow

Over pentagram loomed.

A demon…

Beaming, brightly dark

A spiritual shark

Roaming dimensions

Seeking prey till a spark,

Calls forth its presence

To the present, by peasant

Or maybe a master

Requesting disaster

Or, to kill a bastard

So throne could be had,

Depends what they're after…

In this chapter, re-enactors

Played a scene that had bean

The most major factor

For this town's slate, now clean.

Every full moon

That wakes every month

A portal doth open

Fore Boke must feed up.

Pickings are easy

When folks live in fear

And lately, pure terror

Was abundant round here.

Now, a demon was craving

A feast made of souls

To leave bodies like shells

Taking what made Boke whole…

All the while, not a smile

Did the two hunters sport

No, in fact, stepping back

Showing signs of abort.

Yep, those steps quickened up

And then turned to a run

Down the path they'd retract

Back the same route they'd come.

When their race had returned

The two to the three

This time, they climbed

Up trap door to be free.

Yeah, right….

Not in sight, but in sound

Around corner they heard

The beastly black monster

Shrieked sounds that weren't words.

Back in the lobby,

Main room of the church

Their view drained their flesh

Pale as bark of a birch.

With emerald eyes

And a body of fog

The predator sniffed

Out his food like a dog.

In a moment that felt

Like an eon in time

The fiend found our friends

And then stopped on a dime…

Oh, an alien place

The strange time in space

Where moment of death

Is what you're faced to face.

When music is cut

And sharp notes fall flat

All nine lives done spent

Up in everyone's cat…

It happened so fast

Like lightning in storm

A bottle was filled

While a man's soul was torn.

The boy, only watched

As a barter took place

His father's flushed figure

froze, lifeless… erased.

Though, tight in his hold

A bottle, filled full

An eye-raising bounty

Worth boxes of gold.

Although,

Burns would be cold

And as memories mold

Minds keep inside

Inner demons that scold.

Tho, when outer examples

Are causing for pain,

Traumatization's

A two-sided stain…

"DAD!" The youth screamed

But it fell on deaf ears

Not a trick, fore no smoke

Clouded up any mirrors.

His worst fears had come true

His papa was dead,

Now all he could hope

Up to heaven twas led.

Grief, like a beef

That ends up dead wrong

Or a sad, lonesome verse

From a Hank Senior song.

Teardrops slid down

Off the face of a child

Sure, mission accomplished

But for years, he'd not smile.

Down the old mountain

One walked with stone face

Nothing would heal

Wounds gained in that place…

Tho, Garbool was plum pleased

With this quarry brought due

And so "life damage" costs

Were taken care too.

Now, but an orphan

And no place of his own

A hunter was trained

To fetch ghostly dough.

Calendars flipped

Till an expert was made

Getting rich off of those

Who had rose from the grave.

Each night after day,

Hunters set out

From near and from far

Who, if are not careful

Could live like his dad

And end up, in jar…

# GHOSTS IN JARS III: DEBT SENTENCE

*"Humans are born*

*They live, and they die*

*Tis common routine*

*And nobody knows why.*

*The creek rarely strays*

*From its one, labeled path*

*It wets the same soil*

*In a cool, constant bath.*

*But the long, heavy rain*

*Maybe soon, maybe not*

*Will fall on the stream*

*Swelling same path to rot.*

*Though, just as the sky*

*Lay waste to the flow*

*Its sun zaps the spill*

*Giving birth to new roads.*

*Every man, every woman*

*Every boy, every girl*

*Has one flowing path*

*And whose ever meets ours,*

*That's the stuff of your world."*

"Hmm…" thought a girl

As she closed up the book

Then a bite from her toast

A young lady did took.

Her father's library

Filled with novels and smells

Dust, must, and mice

Looked down from high shelves.

Stories of heroes,

Their steeds and their blades

Long tomes of poems

With a verse on each page.

Romance, a drama

Books bound large and small

If a reader, you were

Than this place had it all…

With the sound of the pounds

From feminine feet

One hit the last step

Thus, ending the beat.

Quick as a whistle

She flew down the hall

In the yard, mom and rooster

Were both making calls.

The mother's? For chores

The rooster's? No reason

He clucked and he'd strut

As he did what he's pleasin'.

A basket for eggs

And a bucket for water

Two tools for the trade

That her mother had brought her.

A steady, sure grip

Makes for green, garden veggies

But a swift, hen-peck dodge

Makes for egg theft a-plenty…

At these same, morning tasks

Her skill had grown grand

So, as fitting for these

She received a small hand.

With the plants having drank

And the chickens been robbed

A kid made allowance

From the days done well jobbed.

Their miniscule farm

Smack-dab in a shire

Made of mill yards and fields

Chopped in squares by barbed wire…

But just up the road

Then just down the way

A few scattered shops

Was the place merchants played.

"Play?" you ask

"Just how do you mean?"

Well, first you must tread

Where a swindler has been.

In most modern times

Ya'll have men who sell cars

And if verbal scat flew

They could soar to the stars.

By this, I do state

That well, lies they would spit

And spit they'd do often

Because lies taste like shit.

Every day, similar folk

Would rather to gather up here

To see if good luck, could get them a buck

And fill up their bellies with beer…

But fate never waits

For people to move

As it searches for someone to come,

And destiny cares, not even a bit

If that do-er is crafty or dumb.

Infant or old

Female or dude

Quiet or loud

Boldish or prude.

A change would be made

In the life of a girl

On a trek she would go

Off, into the world.

Strings would be pulled

And a tapestry spun

Till weaves from a quilt

Made of quest were all done…

As one wandered amongst the crowd

A vase was placed for sale,

And for whatever reason

Or whatever season

Toward it, one's wind, caught sail.

Never before that store she'd been

But liked the price on tag

Hopefully, that porcelain piece

She could haggle to be bagged.

With a creak and a smack

A dingy hinge closed

As she glared at the wares

That were set up in rows.

A shuffle was heard

Probably made by the rat

Dashing fast, but behind

There chased a large cat.

The rodent, met its mouth

And some razer-sharp teeth

After paws were licked clean

Claws sank back in sheath.

The girl, she looked on

As the tabby curled up

On a huge, wooden chest

That was covered in stuff.

Then a black hatch flew open

As a shape limped inside

With a wretched hooked nose

And two olive-like eyes…

Air would go in

Then choked, and coughed out

While if sick had a smell

He would reek of ripe gout.

She hadn't a clue

Or reason for why

But she walked right up

Looking straight in his… eye.

Yes, one orb was glass

The other was real

One darted and scanned

One sat stiff as steel.

"What do I owe,

This pleasure?" he hissed

"A lady, like you

In my muddled abyss?"

She searched, but alas

No words could be found

Then our lass stopped and stared

Looking down at the ground…

"Well?" He did ask

"What could be that you want?

Little lingering brat,

Filling space in my haunt."

But she was a child

Aged no more than twelve

So he'd make her day

Walking back to blacked shelves.

Posted in shadows

In the shack's farthest far

Sat a covered, container

Leather-bound-up old jar.

With a swoop and a swipe

And a dust sweeping wipe

He'd again picked a pear

That was years beyond ripe…

Like a champions trophy

He raised it above

Twas his favorite possession

And the last thing he loved…

Well, that and salted gobies

His breath stank rank of fish

And every time, his lungs would whine

Huge whiffs of fish you'd sniff.

Tho, eyes filled with youth

Looked bored, and confused

"Surely" She thought

"his mind is wrought,

And most his screws are loose."

Oh, but they were

…without a doubt

A minds all but lost

A five-hundred-year bout…

He was Garbool

And the oldest of men

Still selling junk

As folk started, and went.

But hidden inside

Lay a gem from the past

Of an age long ago

# When his business kicked ass…

The hide was removed

As he held it up close

And a moving mist wailed

Twas indeed, but a ghost!

She couldn't believe

Eyes must be deceived

A spirit entrapped

With no options for leave?

In a book, at the farm

She once read a tale

Of hunters who'd chase

And then place ghosts for sale.

They'd travel the land

And its haunted locations

Lurk up some souls,

Then return to their stations.

But that was made law

Or rather, against…

Traditions then ceased

No more phantoms were fenced…

"The good days"

Garbool sighed, as he said

"When the living made bank

Off the ranks of the dead…

This, is the last

Go on have a peek

And fear, you must not

Fore this antique won't leak."

So she pressed up her eyes

On the ancient, old glass

Then fright turned to guilt

And the shame wouldn't pass.

It shrieked in her face

But in grief, not in rage

As this moment, it seemed

Put her up on some stage…

The next thing she knew

Her hands snapped and snatched

As Garbool's eyes went wide

Cuz, she loosened the hatch.

"Pop!" Went the top

To a weathered, old jar

Then the prisoner ran

I mean, floated, afar.

"NOOO!" Screamed Garbool

"How dare you, I say!

I share my one treasure…

And you throw it away!?!"

Fuming snorts he retorted,

Rationale long deported

While a murderous scowl

His jowls, surely sported.

Stepping back in the corner

Past boxes and crates

A scared, child fled

From one's anger and hate…

But you can't run forever

When to shorten a race

Is an obstructed course

That has run out of space.

The curses that flew

Shooting spit from his mouth

Sprinkled and sprayed

Like a broke, drooling spout.

Though, just when it seemed

His rage would explode

She pointed above,

Then quietly spoke.

"Look, at the sign

Ill follow your rule."

As the rusty gears turned

In the brain of Garbool.

Fore nailed in the wall

Was a written-on tin

And the spark to the match

Fore which quest would begin…

It read:

*"Any mask, any flask*

*Any chest, any vase*

*If smash it you do*

*Then YOU shall replace"*

"I'll get you another!"

She told the old wretch

"A ghost in a jar,

I'll just have to fetch."

Then a wicked idea

Matched a devilish grin

"Alright!" Garbool snapped

"Now let us begin!"

So he walked to the back

And yanked off a sheet

Revealing a box

Sealing tools she would need.

Inside were some jars

But he'd give her just one

Cuz a deal was a deal

To redo, the undone.

Around the top was a rope

Golden fibers wound tight

Blessed by the pope

Locked a spirit up right.

Also, a cross

For something to hold

And a white goat's skin cloak

Cuz the mountains were cold…

Fore high hills a yonder

Were the best spots to find

A lost, hiker's ghost

That was out of its mind.

Or remains of a miner

Crushed dead in a cave

Though he'd prayed to be safe

Only soul would be saved…

"Yes, a novice could snatch

Those most wimpy ghosts

To the Capps you will go

Then return to this post.

When a specter you spot

Open up, and give shout

JAR, TRAP THIS FIEND

AND DON'T LET IT OUT!"

"Sounds easy to me"

She said with a smirk

"Then, out of my sight!"

Snapped Garbool, "Get to work!'

Just an hour before

She'd come to this place

With a couple of coins

To purchase a vase.

Now, in a web

And stuck to the sides

With the only way out

Was to go on this ride…

So she wandered back home

And it took her till night

But no spark in the dark

Marks a trail with no light.

It was quarter past one

When the door to her home

Opened, and in

Came our small, beardless gnome.

Her mother, was waiting

By a candle lit bright

Hoping for daughter's

Return from this flight.

Tears of relief

Flowed, soaking her eyes

As the worrisome stress

Almost caused her to die.

But a bath and a snack

Marked the end to this day

When most mortals sleep

And the poltergeists play…

With sparrow made chirps

Bed covers were tossed

Leaving her quarters

Like teeth left not flossed.

"Yes, mother will rant"

She thought, "but who cares?"

Cuz smells of adventure

Lay thick in the air.

Every kid on the Earth

Their minds, give its best

Attempt to conjure

A fantastic quest.

To fly in the clouds

On back of a dragon

Or cross the great plains

In an old, covered wagon.

Imagine…. Please…

But here, on this day

Would begin her big trek

To escape these same fields,

And woods of her neck.

She stepped through a thicket

Past brambles and thorns

Tho, a vine caught her side

And her tunic was torn.

Next, a canteen

Cuz you must have fresh water

Fore thirst is the worst

If hill monsters ain't caught her.

Stories were told

By the ones in her village

Of beasts who'd descend

Upon them and pillage.

"Only tall tales"

She surely did hope

To be captured by them

One would not want to cope...

A few chunks of cheese

And a half loaf of bread

While compass was checked

For direction to head.

Coupled with gear

She'd obtained from Garbool

It seemed that she had

Every required tool...

"Scurry away,

And fly from the house!

Before mom locks up

With me in, and not out."

A zig-zaggy path

That wrapped through the trees

Were quickly consumed

By fast, choppy knees.

Soon, a half mile

Between her and home

Then she thought of the note

Left to parents, in poem.

*"Dearest, Parents dearest"*

It redundantly read

*"Fear not, though I may*

*Just might wind up dead.*

*I've gone on a journey*

*With the wild as my host*

*To the Gandolin Capps*

*And I'm seeking a ghost,*

*I encountered a cretin*

*By name of Garbool*

*Then a fast, ghastly break*

*Forced my debt to that fool.*

*So a cross country quest*

*Holding one holy bottle*

*Time to prove, to myself*

*That I ain't been too coddled.*

*If I don't make it back*

*My one final wish*

*Is that no tears are shed*

And P.S… feed my fish" …

But mother, straight freaked

After reading those words

And her apish like howls

All around could be heard.

Then all through the county

A "please find my" bounty

On bulletin boards were in place,

No doubt folks in town

Would gather their hounds

In a, "let's find her first!" kind of pace.

A handsome reward

Of a hundred gold bars

To be scored, by the horde

Who saves kin of Lorde Mars.

Even though they were royals

To be humble, he'd taught her

A nice thing to see

From the Deputy's daughter…

A map to the hills

Surveyed by Garbool

Showed all the old roads,

Twas her GPS fuel.

But cartography alters

When new trails are blazed

As ancient trade routes

Form a quite faded maze…

Four miles north

Then two miles west

As mounds became hills

And the trees became less.

She came to a farm

With a red barn on ridge

While her canyon-cross path

Twas a rickety bridge.

A scraggly chicken

Its squawks rang aloud

With bird brains indeed

Seemed foolishly proud.

She felt for the bird

Cuz its foot had been tethered

With reptile eyes

And thinning, black feathers.

"Why is this rooster,

Tied up alone?

Leash-bound to the ground

While no one's at home?"

As she stepped closer

Her ears swore they heard

Not poultry-made clucks

But actual words!

Yes, where normal bird-banter

Would usually be

This creature was screeching

First, "Help!" and then, "me!" …

Confusion, then fright

Came over her quick

Tho courage, not coward

Was what she would pick.

Five feet from the place

The chicken's chain reached

Stood our young, questing kid

Who was finding no speech.

It had been two full weeks

Since its breast had seen rest

Fore beaked-ones wont sleep

Where there isn't a nest...

"Under that rock!"

It pointed and hissed

"Lies a key, made of brass

That your eyes couldn't miss!"

Then hands heaved a boulder

Oh which the voice spoke

"Am I losing my mind?

Cuz this must be a joke!"

Though, strange as it seemed

There sat in the sand

A small, metal pick

That she scooped in her hand.

Then careful advances

Toward a gnarly old bird

As it flapped its wings up

It mixed caws with cursed words…

A click and a snap

And a lock was unlatched

With a toss in the grass

That leash was made past.

Now free, in the air

Up the beast hovered

But reasons for gab

Hadn't yet been uncovered.

"Do all chickens speak?"

The child charge uttered

"Till times of great need

Do they keep their tongues under?"

"No!" said the rooster

"I'm human inside,

Tho my soul, and this poultry

Are caught in a bind."

"My name is Garbanzo

This farm, was my post

But along came hill creatures

And then, we were toast.

My people were slaughtered

Our livestock were rustled

I tried to be strong

But we just got out-muscled.

During the battle

A blade struck my neck

And that once talking head

Was then rolling on deck.

Then a terrible warlock

By name of Rahmeel

Cast forth a horrible spell,

With throated notes sung

In more than one tongue

He summoned an agent of hell.

As weird as it seemed

This unlikely team

Of necro-mancer and monsters,

Quickly dispersed

When a shadow so cursed

Turned, the bizarre into bonkers.

A demon, called Yagg

Appeared on a crag

As greenish-black haze swirled around,

Then this tardy soul

Got stuck in my skull

Till Yagg smelled me out

And screamed loud…"

"Send this fool's spirit

Searching about

Till the first beastly host

Save our steeds,

He hath found!" ...

"Then a spark, and a sputter

As the universe stuttered

And Yagg disappeared in a blink,

Myself on the other

Hand, oh brother

Felt like a rag in the sink.

Cold...

Most frigid I felt

You've never been dead

So you clearly ain't dealt.

Plus, it does seem

That my soul stinks at pickin'

Cuz the dang thing flew near

And then into this chicken!

I'm sickened.

So, I have chilled

alone on this hill

Since Rahmeel stuck me still

To the place we were killed…"

The bird then looked up

With a sad pair of eyes

Two scarred orbs who'd spied

His tribes' final cries.

"I need to cross over."

Garbanzo said low

"To meet my sweet clan

At wherever ghosts go."

But how it would happen,

Neither would know

As an exit was made

With a new friend in tow…

Over the next,

Few hours spent walking

The girl and the undead

Zombird kept talking.

Meanwhile, hunters

With dreams of a bounty

Had spread over each

Every part of the county.

Packs upon packs

Of bloodhounds caught scent

That were bought from an Aunt

At her flea market tent.

The socks from her niece

Could now fetch a fortune

Five hundred and two

Jagaroons, each per portion.

Yep, that kind of business

Deserves a diploma

Stacking that cash

Off of stinky aromas.

In fact,

The boots

The shirts

The dresses

The skirts,

All were now pawned

With her tradeoff in purse.

If things got to worst

And they'd need them a hearse

At least she made bank

From her plan she'd thought first…

What a selfish, (curse) …

As a middle-aged lady

Made profits from stockings

A babe and a bird

Couldn't find phantoms flocking.

Much walking, much stalking

Tho shows were not rocking

The rooster kept belting

His frustrated squawking.

"I was the only

Ghost in this valley!?!

I watched scores of my friends

All die in high tally!"

The night brought the black

But an orange flame burned bright

Lone, beacon of light

On their foothill campsite.

Except for the moon

Making arc in the sky

Anti-dark satellite

Floating in-flight white pie.

Young eyes open wide

Gawked in awe at the sight

The largest of lunars

She'd seen in her life.

Canines a plenty

Their howls heard afar

Didn't hijack the thoughts

Of a kid with a jar…

She woke right at dawn

To appropriate caws

Shrieked by a feathered companion,

It just happened so

That a one rooster's crow

Was a trait, that was cross-species spannin'.

He'd also discovered

His love for uncovered

Crickets and spiders and grubs,

But the part twas most tight

Were the short bursts of flight

He would use to reach perches above.

"These fingers, they'll fit"

The rooster did spit

Tho the love, was surely short-lived,

With darker emotions

Than the depths of the oceans

His hatred would leak, like a sieve...

"Lord, PLEASE get me out!"

He one day did shout

After stubbing his claw on a root,

"This violent toe tappin'

Wouldn't have happened

If my feet, could still scoot in boots!"

Of course, she would laugh

At his avian rage

But soon, matters would, take a turn

Fore inches between

Where they'd go

And they'd been

Grew shorter each day, which they'd learn.

First, through the pines

Then crossing the canyon

To water they saw

Near a grand stand of banyans.

Where gigantic mountains

Rose high in their vision,

A freshly found fork

Would require decision...

"I say we go left!"

Yelled the boldly brained bird,

But his voice, and its choice

Held wisdom less words.

After just half a mile

They came upon pile

Of hill monster victims

Their bodies... defiled.

While the god awful stench

Could wrench vultures to smile

Our duo, disgusted

By wafts, awfully vile.

That scene would have made

Any eyes nice and sore

So they turned themselves back

And away from the gore...

At return to the split

This time, they chose right

In more ways than one

Because up in their sight,

A winding up path

Scaling faces of rock

Like a Mount Rushmore road

Made of Abe Lincoln's snot.

Higher they climbed
With each passing step
Till they'd got them to where
Only mountain goats trekked.

Soon, the trail's neck
Seemed to bottle up tight
As below, floated clouds
Puffy pillows of white.
Yes, these holy heights
Had seen falls, and fights
And lives cast tasting
Those dusty-tongued bites…

The gusty winds whispered,
Minty-fresh breaths of zephyr

My-oh-my, mountains sure

Have some dangerous weather.

As the sun went to bed

And the stars dotted dark

Two travelers crashed

Now, near their mark.

Lying up ahead a mile

Massive, onyx colored piles

And hopefully, haunted mines

In their gloomy, winding style…

That morning the pouring

Of rain, soaked their bones

Fogging the focus

Of minds in a zone.

Yes, misery lurks

In the cold, soggy shadows

When damp turns to frost

And dry socks, they had no.

Grins of the past

Had converted to frowns

As the air dropped in temp

And the torrents came down.

Yet, upward they scaled

Cuz when you are "that" close

The joy of met goals

Will out-weigh the morose…

A polar exhale

Hexed with speckles of hale

Greeted our weary-eyed souls,

But now, near the peak

They drank from the creek

Whose flows made for water, so cold.

But wind-burns soon sweltered

So, step one was shelter

To keep their conditions from worse,

Dripped drops and two "slaps!"

Made sound as laid-back

Travelers dropped and plopped first.

In a cavern, of course

With no room for a horse

Like a mini garage forced

To hold one, petitely posh Porsche.

Ole Goldilocks, she

Would've laughed at the sight

"For myself, much too tight"

But for them, twas just right…

\*\*\*\*\*\*\*\*\*\*\*\*\*\*\*\*\*

The gems in the hills

Over much blood is spilled,

Humans are hooked

And for looks, they will kill.

Below, near the base

Where the rats quickly raced

With hamster wheels powered by dogs,

A most ragged creep

Whose empty stare seeped,

Panted and wheezed as he jogged.

Held firm in his hand

The key to his plan,

A two time bathed in blood dagger,

He mumbled along

To a terrible song

Mos Def not a pitch perfect bragger.

This howling hound herder

Resorted to murder

To better his odds for the chase,

Twin homicides

Of which, he would lie

Or face, a big fall from grace…

Twenty-three teams

One week past, made leave

And since, two now departed

Because a soul, blackened

knife-man named Mack

Made sure, they'd been discarded.

Still, no signs

Or clues had been found

Who knew if that girl's

On the world, still around?

But the prize was so grand

He'd win or die trying,

"I'd never go back

To that royal house spying!"

Yes, he had spent

A number of years

Slinking and snooping

For rumors and fears.

Gathering info

For a king far away

And once, he was caught

But he killed, and escaped…

Then home, he returned

Tho cast out and spurned

For treacherous treason took part,

Betrayal by those

With same crest on their clothes

Destroyed what remained of his heart.

So, after old Mack

Swore not to go back

He knew, that if he did find,

The royalty's kin

He'd have to go in

That damn, awful castle's inside.

Days dragged along

And his rations wore thin

The nights, were quite cold

And the days, hot as sin...

\*\*\*\*\*\*\*\*\*\*\*\*\*\*\*\*\*\*\*\*\*\*

While men in the night

Kept the search up for treasure

A child and chicken

Dodged terrible weather.

Under skies with no moon

Or stars to give clues

They chose to make sense

Of Garbool's scribbled runes.

After much study

And scans of the page

No progress was made

Beyond the first stage.

\*\*\*\*\*\*\*\*\*\*\*\*\*\*\*\*\*\*\*\*\*

\*\*\*\*\*\*\*\*\*\*\*\*\*\*\*\*\*\*\*\*

Back in the shack

A geezer grinned wide,

As a gold jagaroon

His molar did bite.

A peddling meddler, swindled supreme

"Ahh, gents with no sense

Loose their cents

Like a dream…

It's almost obscene…"

Garbool beamed from his scheme

Yes, in most recent scene

He'd treated a chump

To some "magical beans."

"Legumes of the gods"

He pitched to his victim

"Just go plant them once,

And you won't have to pick them!

They fly off the stalk

And harvest themselves

Then, before you know

They're up on your shelves!"

Rumors had swirled around, town as of late

And of who, would locate

The Lorde's little lass

Twas heated debate.

Rambling, gambling men of the town

Met at the pub, and cash was thrown down.

Garbool, was aware

He had risked a fair sum

Fore two of the teams…

Yup, under his thumb.

He funded some trackers

With coins he could ditch

If winners, they were

Five fiends would be rich.

Most people would think

"My goodness, you're sick!"

Though our merchant would say

"Oppur-tu-nis-tic."

Patient he was,

for results to see

"Woops…my bad, child…"

He'd given her…

The wrong, M-A-P…

\*\*\*\*\*\*\*\*\*\*\*\*\*\*\*\*\*\*\*\*\*\*\*

\*\*\*\*\*\*\*\*\*\*\*\*\*\*\*\*\*\*\*\*\*\*\*\*\*\*\*

"How will I meet, this challenge?

I'm beat...

A novice ghost hunter now cried,

"Garbool said this map

Could guide through the Capps

But I think that fool mighta lied."

Then, she leaned back

To "creeeak" and a crack

Below, a rope severed

And trap door done levered.

"Ahh!" filled the air

Loud shouts from her mouth,

Diving through darkness

Can make one, fall south.

"Thud!" was the sound

Made by the pound


When one human found

Their self on the ground.

"Ouch!" She whined

Hand rubbing her head

Then noticed the scuff

On her arm, which now bled.

Thin streams of red

Dripped drops on the dirt

Falls, from twenty-five feet

Often hurt...

Garbanzo looked down

"Hey kid, you alright?"

She groaned as he floated

Toward her in flight.

"Now, we must find

Our way through these caves…"

Where many got lost

And had made them their graves.

In need of some light

They were, in exactness

So that navigation

Could be done, in the blackness.

A solution was found

In the eyes of a rooster

Which shined ghostly white

Quite the, morale booster

His optical orbs

Flared up like a lamp

So vision was made

In the dark and the damp.

From tunnel to tunnel

They scurried along

As two singing sets

Of their footsteps made song.

Minutes formed hours

As on they kept walking

But with no end in sight

They continued their stalking.

"Why do you stay?"

The girl asked the bird

Tho the poultry said nothing,

Not one single word.

"Answer me, chicken!"

This, more a demand…

That caused abrupt halting

On uncharted land.

"I'm here for your safety,"

He chirped through his beak

As far up ahead,

They heard something squeak…

Foul fumes, then rose

Quickly filling the air

So potent, in fact

They became tough to bare.

"Oh my soul!" Snarled the minor

Holding hand up to nose

"I will barf on my scarf

If those fumes onward, grow!'…

Shortly, there after

Lights far up ahead,

Framed green, darting glares

Sharing no shadow's tread.

The dead…

Blurred out image that bled,

To say "hey, they're living…"

Is giving way, too much cred.

A spiritual scene

A limbo of sorts

Down in this underground,

Centralized court.

Now, they could see

Five paths came together

Forming a chamber

Immune from the weather.

Crystallized cavern

With pillars of stone,

Held no holes above

Of which sun, could be shown…

Torches were lit

And their faces were hit,

By light, that was hue

Of a sailor's seen sick.

Green, not with envy

But somber and sad

Emerald aura

That came across bad.

Picking, and digging

And working away

Since they had died

In that mode they did stay.

Frozen, like water drops

Stopped… Cuz when temps flop

Cold is a solid soul

Pulled from husk, post-crop…

Their faces looked hurried

And well, out of breath

When the hustle don't stop

Even after one's death.

Then, came the moment

Finally, now!

Two hands opened glass

And then shouted out loud…

"Jar, trap this fiend

And don't let it out!"

A wicked wind whipped,

Crackled and ripped

With force to send north

Even largest of ships.

It hissed,

But just as its target got hit… it quit

Though, ate up the dust

Of which dust had been bit.

It fit.

Now, floating and bottled

Non-alcohol spirit

Screams could be heard

Yet, neither them feared it.

One of course,

Was part phantom himself

Though as poltergeist poultry go,

This bird was top shelf…

The little one didn't know

Not to be brave

When you're too young to think

Things weren't always that way.

Hadn't seen much

Of the struggle and grind

The daily routine

That can drown what's inside.

Keep adventure alive…

Footsteps then rang

Coming up from behind

Two looked and were greeted

By a haggard in line.

Flashing eyes so erratic

He spoke so emphatic

"I found her! I found her

At last!"

Things had looked up

For old Mack indeed

From awful, to awesome quite fast.

"You are the child

Of the duke, are you not?

I… watched you do witchcraft

Saw that ghost that you caught!"

She then formed a puzzled

Look seen in her eyes

"Witchcraft?" she thought

"Surely, he lies."

Tho, held in her grasp

The phantom in jar

And reasoning for

From home, she was far.

Old Mack had heard tales

But he thought them just myths

Now, he was witness

To this young, little witch…

Garbanzo stood back

Only clucking in role

Then analyzed eyes

That seemed wretched and cold.

"We have to get rid

Of this man, yes we must,

Leave him behind

Left to choke on our dust.

Oh, I do not trust

A man whose glare burns

With backs he hath stabbed

Till it comes to our turn…"

The three hands, turned right

And clockwork twas tickin'

Pickin' his brain

Was our de-tec-tive chicken.

The man, hadn't ate

In nearly two days

Now… with this bird

A meal would be made.

He whipped out his blade

Then spoke rather sultry,

"I'm cravin' carved-shavin'

White meat from that poultry."

Garbanzo jumped back

As a dagger sliced close,

"No!" The girl screamed,

"That's my feathered pet ghost!"

"Nonsense!" Mack yelled

"Your mind is a mess…"

His stare, was transfixed

On the rooster's plump breast.

The result, was quite sad

He'd gone mad…

After days of exhaustion

And having no food

Plus, effects on your mind

From killing five dudes,

Screws were loose…

Spitting and waving

He stumbled about,

As words of some prize

From his mouth, he did shout.

But simply, no matter

Which words had come out

His sanity now

Was much more than, "In doubt."

Garbanzo dodged left

Then swerved to the right

With margins between

Him and knife were quite tight.

Then, with a stab

The blade found its mark

Yet no blood was spilled

On that cave in the dark.

Even though, deep below

His flesh, slid the edge

No damage was done

By that thin, metal wedge…

"What trick is this now!?!"

Asked Mack in such wonder

"This bird should be done

Fore my dagger sunk under!"

But Garbanzo, stayed up

With no feathers red

Even he himself shocked

That he wasn't now dead.

"I guess when that demon

From out of that portal

Cursed me like this,

He made me… immortal."

A chortle,

Came sliding through beak

Not a human like laugh

Though it caused Mack to freak.

"This chicken's a ghoul,

A golem of evil!

I must see it vanquished

For good of all people!"

In a flash of true madness

He threw down his knife

Proceeding to lunge

In attempt to take life…

The girl, looked on

At this scene so bizarre

Her feet, sticking still

As if muck-stuck to tar.

A hole in the floor

With no bottom showing,

I think you can see

Where this poem, will be going.

The pace of the chase

Only hastened, not slowing

As that chasm so deep

Our Garbanzo was knowing…

He clucked, then he jumped

As he flew through the air

As two flailing snares

Kept on coming up bare.

Then, the trap set

As scaly legs landed

Mack looked down… and found

Not on ground, had he standed.

"Bloody Hell!" was the yell

That was heard for a while

Till an imminent "thud"

Meant a new, lifeless pile…

Then two, caught their breath

Bodies covered with sweat

Still not sure what was next

Cuz, they'd just caused a death!

Then calmness they found

When lights all around

Seemed to flicker an arrow of sorts,

Though not knowing why

Follow, they'd try

Maybe now, get on, exit course.

Back through the mountain

Down steep, granite stairs

Passing rock-chiseled

Stone-whittled black chairs.

Torches were hung

But no wicks were lit

Strangely the lights

Not in fuel did they sit.

Still, not one question

They bothered to ask

To follow these wisps

Was their most crucial task.

Bats glided past

Shrieking and flying

Never once crashing

Without ever trying.

Hours dragged on

As the arrow shone still

Dancing and blazing

Till dark, the lights killed…

Our worms tunneled long

Winding through earth

As mysterious wisps

Gave a hopeful rebirth.

"I've had my fill!"

Garbanzo whined loud

"Who's to say we ain't lost?

We will never get out!"

Though foresight, not keen

This time in our bird

Cuz five minutes later

He'd feast on his words.

For the first time in days

The sun found their skin

As a hole in the wall

Of the cave, made for grins…

"I knew if we trailed

These orbs, we'd be free!"

The girl rolled her eyes

As the bird clucked with glee.

Indeed, they saw trees

And grass in the breeze

Heard buzzing from dozens

Of dozens of bees.

They thanked their new friends

Every last ball of glow,

Then drank from the stream

Which now nearby flowed…

"Where do we head?"

One wondered aloud

As cold, liquid drops

Fell on down from the clouds.

However, quite careless

They seemed as they walked

Smiles took place

Of words they could talk.

Just happy to stroll

In the world above ground

Oh, silence is gold

When joy rings without sound.

Miles through forest

O'er prairies and fields

With staff in one's hand

And bottle in wield.

Trapped in the glass

That ghastly green miner

Splayed and pressed up

To that jar's see-through liner…

Desperate for direction

With location not known

So they wandered along

Like a leaf in gusts blown.

"All for some debt?

Wow, you have honor"

But weight on her back

Was no longer upon her.

After an eon

A village drew near

And the sight of this civ

Spread their grins ear-to-ear.

Houses and fires,

Drunk laughter and songs

Since last these scenes saw

It had been awfully long…

A poster nailed high

On the wall of a shop

Caught eyes of our duo

Then caused jaws to drop.

*"Wanted: For Murder"*

Then plastered in place

A raggedly haggard

Familiar face.

Twas the same man they saw

Then tricked to a fall

Truly "swift justice"

Their act could be called,

But they…were appalled.

"Oh my god, we'll be next!"

Cackled the cock

Then wheeled right around

And into more shock.

Nailed to a tree

Read another pinned sign:

*"Hefty Reward:*

*For the one who does find."*

Under the offer

The face of a lass

"Oh my" the girl sighed

"I must get home fast!"

...

They knew where to go

With a map as their clue

So southward they went

One on claws, one in shoes.

All though the night

They walked down the road

Toward Gandolin City

Where the king sat on throne…

"Why you no tell me,

You're of royal blood?"

Asked a dirty old rooster

Who was covered in mud.

"It never occurred."

She answered right back,

But Garbanzo thought

Of this sheer lack of facts.

*"Six miles ahead"*

Said a marker of towns

On edge of the path

They'd been marching down.

Morning lark whistles

Marked breaking of day,

The capital, close

As they marched on their way.

From wilderness route

To houses and farms

To brick, office halls

Chiming hanging door charms…

The last time Garbanzo

Had been to this place,

Was to barter his bulls

When he wore a man's face.

A castle loomed large

Against urban backdrop

A council they sought

With whom, sits on top.

Arriving at noon

They gawked at some guards

Who messed with and pestered

A most, wasted bard.

"Beat it!" They screamed

"Your tunes are off pitch!"

They then pushed him down

And into a ditch…

"Leave him alone!"

The girl barked with rage

As a spotlight shone down

Propping her up on stage.

"Just who do you think,

You are?" said a man

"I'm the daughter of Lorde

Mars of the West Lands!"

Their jaws fell agape

As awe coursed throughout

"I thought you were dead!"

One fat soldier did shout.

"Well no, I am not

My death's not a thing

Now please, if we may

Can we speak with the king?"

An escort was made

And their entrance prepared

Cuz denying lorde's kin

Is a bad way to fare.

They were rushed through the court

And swept past the ballast

From basement to palace

From bone mug, to gold chalice…

"I NEED salted pork!

No damn beef will do!"

A bearded man scolded

A chef and his crew.

The food makers ran

To fetch flesh of swine

For feast of the season

Which nobles would dine.

The ruler supreme

Of the land, Gandolin

Had an appetite, not quite light

To begin.

He'd swallow whole meal

Then follow, with veal

Could ingest spoiled flesh

With his stomach of steel.

Governing body,

And his was so large

If push weight 'round you must,

It made sense him in charge.

After screaming and stomping

And ranting with ire

He whirled when he heard

A young voice say, "Sire?"

Surprise filled his eye

"My dear," he shot back

Just whom on the chase

You down, did they track?"

Fore surely, he cared

The Lorde's spawn was spared!

Tho two, umm… "paid-aids"

"The hunt" had they dared.

Now, he would find

Just who'd won the pot
Of which, had grown large
And worth quite a lot…

"No one, my liege
I found my way here"
The king only nodded
Then drank from his beer.
"It shall be known
That you've returned safe…
Tell Lorde Mars at once!
She's no longer a waif!"
A message was sent
And within a week,
Her father rode up
On a dark horse, so sleek.

A smile so wide

Unveils the disguise

Of joy, seeping out

In the tears that soaked eyes.

Embraced with a hug,

But she never once told

The reasons she'd left

While Garbool… hadn't yet, out been sold.

Garbanzo grew restless

His fate, not yet know

Nervously wandered

As impatience had grown.

Pacing and grazing

On bugs in the rug

The strings to his heart

Were then tightly tugged…

"Father, my chicken

He must come on home."

The king, only sipped

Beard frosty with foam.

"If that be your wish

We'll bring on this bird"

A cluck of elation

Was then quickly heard.

Handshakes were shook

And steeds were prepared,

With custom roost saddle

Garbanzo would share…

A "short" travel later

The West Lands were seen,

A while had passed

Since this place she'd bean.

Familiar pathways

Burnt deep in one's mind

Paint themselves bright

Even when long behind.

Lush, fields of green

And meadows of gold

Big, friendly trees

And little creeks, cold.

Her neighbors waved arms

And shouted her name,

After such a fuss raised

She had flamed up some fame.

Tho, as far as they knew

She'd been lost and found

Nobody knew reasons

For her leaving town…

As a happy black rooster,

Most likely a bantam

Sounded his call

One peeked at her phantom.

Swirling and churning

The mist in the jar

Festered in place

Like an infected scar…

Their horses stopped still

In midst of the street

Fore a brown, coiled snake

Lay down at beasts' feet.

It hissed, and then slithered

Back in the grass

A tug on the reins

Started steeds back up fast.

Only one half a mile

Between them and home

Twas back to the bubble

Toward long since seeds sown.

Five minutes later

Their stallions stopped

And mother ran fast

As feet from mount dropped...

Mom, dad, and child

They shared an embrace

As the ride-a-long rooster

Peered at poultry pad place.

"My dear, we've been sick"

The matriarch snapped

"I know mommy, tho

I set my own trap."

Head scratching, they stood

Confusion on face

Then quick as one could

"Gotta go!" As she raced.

Left in her dust

Shocked, still as cement

As Garbanzo took role

Of a flock filled with hens…

Rapidly flashing

"Downtown" toward the shops

Back to the shack

With dark scene, back drop.

Same cat in the corner

Same dust in the air

Yes, much hadn't changed

In this swindler's lair.

Eyes dancing, and glancing

She spotted the fiend

Who on an odd pod

Made of skin, he did lean.

Tinkering fingers

Lingered over a trinket,

Found two separate chains

Connected, and linked it.

Twas then he did sense

A presence within,

When noticed just who

He flashed a big grin…

"Darling, my girl!

You really came back!

A little bit floored

I stand here, as fact."

Tho smile was worn

His wretched brain clicked

"She better have gotten

That which does the trick."

Then out of her bag

Pulled out was a jar

Ghastly green fog

Meant that one passed the bar.

"Well, you have done it

The task, it is run

Tho caused me some dough

From a gambling sum."

Indeed, when the news

Swept all through the land

The pot was split up

Amongst many hands.

"Your debt has been paid

And honor been saved

By snatching that batch

Solo ghost from the grave"

Garbool had heard plenty

About her long quest,

Given talk of the town

Was the most treasured chest.

Tho, no team received

That bounty of cash

Her self-reappearance

Meant Lorde Mars kept his stash.

Greedy teeth gnashed

As his conscious spoke up

"Alright… if you say,

I'll pay this young pup."

A miserly soul

It argued with guilt

But balance of morals

Toward good, this time tilt…

GARBOOL

"I guess I've gone soft"

Said the withered, old loon

"Here, for your trouble

Take five jagaroon."

She'd never expected

To ever get paid,

Tho, when she was handed

Money, smile splayed.

"Thank you Garbool!"

The lass shrieked with glee

"Now can I buy

That vase oh-so green?"

This made the baron

Laugh, slapping his knee

"Ha! For you dear

This one time, it's free!"

She thanked the old bag

Then left on her way

Back to the farm

Where her head would soon lay.

Her parents were waiting

And when she walked in

They then quickly asked,

"Now, where have you been?"

"I made a few bucks,

And got you this gift!'

They chuckled a bit

As from fear to joy shift.

The skies opened up

As rains started pouring,

And this, my dear friends

Is the end to this story.

Well… not quite.

\*\*\*\*\*\*\*\*\*\*\*\*\*\*\*\*\*\*\*\*

\*\*\*\*\*\*\*\*\*\*\*\*\*\*\*\*\*\*\*\*

Far off and away

Two wheels squeaked aloud

As from copper spout

A deep purple cloud.

Then, portal wide opened

And a figure stepped out

A cloaked shadowed man

With a blackish beard, stout.

Remember Rahmeel?

The warlock who'd called,

Upon that dark demon

From scratched star of salt.

This was his haven

Hidden lab in a cave

With trusted technician

Goblin, more his slave.

"My pet, you've done well!"

He showered the imp

Then limped toward a table

With signature gimp.

"Soon, I will rule

This land, Gandolin

An army I'll raise

Then my plan will begin!"

He schemed up his dream

To muster a team

Of all the spirits

The whole world had seen.

Necromancers dance magic

From evil bound books

Recipes ripe

For this evil, hex cook.

Wicked shrieks echoed

Laughter, so bad

In store what was more

Only two knew twas had.

Fore standing, behind him

Surrounded by bars

Sat thirty-five thousand

Ghosts… stuck in jars…

# THE END

# ABOUT THE AUTHOR

D.B. Feister was born and raised in Cadillac, Michigan. He spends his time catching fish, writing music, and thinking about bizarre scenarios. He also has a lethal jump shot from three point range and an unhealthy obsession with breakfast cuisine. He has four sisters (Liz, Sarah, Mary, Gen), two parents (Dan, Nell), and an orange cat (Orange Cat). He drives a replica of Sebulba's Pod Racer, and he communicates with plants. He lives in a secluded mountain cabin where he raises ospreys and builds custom wood furniture. He also wants you to read this book. Also, everything from me driving an intergalactic go kart, to my carpentry skills, was a complete lie.

D. B. Feister

# SPECIAL THANKS

Special thanks to my parents for believing in their eccentric son. Also, special thanks to Dr. Seuss, J.R.R. Tolkien, and Bill Watterson for being influential and what not…Also, thanks to Dixon Ticonderoga for crafting the perfect pencil. Also, thanks to Bruce Loper & Will McConnell for helping me finish this book!

Made in the USA
San Bernardino, CA
17 March 2017